Elisabeth Frink

1930 - 1993

sculptures, graphic works, textiles

Elisabeth Frink

sculptures, graphic works, textiles

*exhibitions organised by
Salisbury Festival with the
Edwin Young Trust, Salisbury
and Dorset County Museum,
Dorchester*

Elisabeth Frink:
a certain unexpectedness

Salisbury Library and Galleries
10 May - 7 June 1997

Salisbury Cathedral and Close
22 May - 19 June 1997
curated by Annette Downing

Elisabeth Frink:
man and the animal world

Dorset County Museum
28 June - 23 August 1997

works chosen by John Hubbard
curated by Richard de Peyer
and Annette Downing

Elisabeth Frink with *Seated Man II*, late 1980s

HISCOX plc

fine art insurance

Sponsoring the Salisbury Festival
by providing the insurance of the Elisabeth Frink exhibition

Hiscox plc

leading insurer of fine art and high value homes,

is delighted to sponsor the insurance of the Elisabeth Frink

exhibition in support of the Salisbury Festival and to

highlight the achievements of modern British artists.

ROBERT HISCOX

Contents

Salisbury exhibition

There is a certain unexpectedness in finding a major retrospective of one of Britain's foremost sculptors taking place outside the usual galleries and existing sculpture parks. Yet there is an undeniable rightness in siting this exhibition within the confines of Salisbury's Cathedral Close and the city's Library and Art Gallery, under the auspices of the Salisbury Festival and the Edwin Young Trust.

The Festival was launched in 1973 and has managed to surprise, delight and challenge audiences throughout its 24-year existence. Its programmes have covered a wide spectrum of classical and other music, together with street events, work for children and community projects. Linking all events has been the determination to programme only work of the highest quality and of relevance to the rural city in which the Festival takes place.

This is the first major exhibition which the Festival has brought together. Frink's work has obvious links with the city. Her *Walking Madonna* is permanently sited in the Close, where it continues to provoke strong reactions. Frink herself lived just over the county boundary in Dorset, where her work was created amid the partic- ular landscapes of rural Wessex. And yet she longed for a retrospective exhibition which placed her work among 'a lot of stone - ancient buildings... a place where people walk and go about their daily business.'

We think that Elisabeth Frink would have been pleased with the setting of her work in the Close and the city, where those who knew and loved her, together with those who will come from far and wide, can enjoy the best work of this remarkable sculptor. Thanks are due to many people who have helped in assembling the exhibition, but most especially to its curator, Annette Downing, who has worked tirelessly to bring this extraordinary collection of work together.

Helen Marriage

Director
Salisbury Festival

Preface 2

Dorchester exhibition

When Dorset County Museum added a prize-winning extension to its buildings in 1972, it was for exhibitions such as this. Elisabeth Frink was a dedicated friend and supporter of the Museum and a member of the Exhibitions Committee here for many years until her death. Dorset was in her blood; she knew everyone, seemed to like everyone and combined a natural affinity with country ways and the people and animals that filled it and her imaginings about it. It was natural that she should want to exhibit in the new gallery here and that the County Museum should encourage and support that wish. Elisabeth Frink's exhibition in 1982 was a great artistic success and typically involved Alex Csárky and Elisabeth, not just as makers and shakers but also dogsbodies and navvies too, heaving bronzes and plinths from van to floor and floor to plinth over several days, carefully arranging and rearranging a rich and fruitful encounter between artist and visitor.

The current exhibition was conceived as a local memorial to Elisabeth's support for the Museum over the years and her love of Dorset. John Hubbard, the distinguished artist and friend of Elisabeth's has chosen an animalist theme for the show, mixing her human and animal creations in bronze and on paper in an original and moving way. Wiltshire County Council's Art Curator, Annette Downing, had the vision and deliberation to suggest a second site to exhibit during the 1997 Salisbury Festival that would extend the range of this, a local tribute, to include a wider range of Elisabeth's human figure sculptures. The result has been a collaboration which allows the visitor to see two successive shows in Salisbury and Dorchester, an opportunity to observe Elisabeth Frink's mind at work in two complementary but distinct exhibitions.

It has been a privilege to work with Elisabeth's son, Lin Jammet, with John Hubbard and Annette Downing in this important joint venture which has brought the added benefits of association with the Salisbury Festival. Exhibitions of this sort do not come cheaply and can be done well only with goodwill and generosity on all sides. The current catalogue has been a product of exemplary goodwill and I hope that you, the reader and visitor, will enjoy the careful and painstaking work which has gone into its production.

Richard de Peyer

Curator
Dorset County Museum
The Dorset Natural History
and Archaeological Society

Frink in her studio with the *Tributes*, late 1970s

Acknowledgements

We are indebted to the following people for their help and support of the exhibition:

Lin and Valerie Jammet
The Estate of Elisabeth Frink
Jean Frink
Mrs M Behrens
David Buckland
Mrs K Christopherson
Commercial Union plc
Ken Cook
Mr and Mrs D Cooke
Mr and Mrs R Croft
Mr B Cronan
Canon Jeremy Davies
The Dean and Chapter,
Salisbury Cathedral
Sir Harry Djanogly
The Dorset Natural History
and Archaeological Society
Mary Fedden
Richard Grasby
David Hibberd
Hiscox Syndicates Ltd, Lloyd's of London
Hong Kong Land Company Ltd
Sir Simon Hornby
John Hubbard
Ickworth House and Garden,
The National Trust
Jardine Lloyd Thomson Group
Dr and Mrs I Key
Laurie Lee
Jorge Lewinski
Edward Lucie-Smith
Meridian Sculpture Foundry Ltd
Moodys Removals
Mr and Mrs B Phelan
Bryan Robertson
Andrew Robertson and
the Cathedral Works Dept.
Chris Rule
Mr and Mrs H Stewart
W H Smith Group plc
Wendy Suffield and
The Blandford Gallery
Mr and Mrs C Wintour
Yorkshire Sculpture Park

I met Elisabeth Frink in 1982 at Dorchester, and have long enjoyed and admired her sculptures. It was therefore a great pleasure to be welcomed to her home in Dorset by her son, Lin Jammet, and to step into a place which echoed with her life and work, interests and loves. Whilst preparing the exhibition I came to rely not so much on individual pieces or even the body of works, but on the ideas and feelings that lay behind all that Elisabeth strove to achieve as well as the reactions that I encountered to her work. She is remembered by all her friends with warmth and affection, her laughter and meals are recalled fondly. This exhibition would not have been possible without the support and generosity of all those who loaned works, often cherished within their homes, and the sponsors as well as the many people who shared their recollections of Elisabeth with me.

I found it impossible to experience her sculptures or drawings without becoming aware of her humanist concerns. In an effort to carry her ideas forward it was decided to hold two events amongst her sculptures: readings from the journal *Index on Censorship* alongside the *Tributes*, the heads she dedicated to Amnesty International, and a performance created and acted by teenagers, inspired by human rights issues and produced by Salisbury Playhouse Education Department.

Annette Downing
Art Curator
The Edwin Young Trust,
Wiltshire County Council
and Salisbury Festival

working on the plaster model for *Risen Christ*, Woolland, Dorset, 1992

Foreword

by Canon Jeremy Davies

Towards the end of last year, I was preaching in New York. I wanted to take with me a piece of Salisbury, that at the same time would speak across the ocean. I wanted to take something of such human seriousness that might provide an immediate rapport between me and my American listeners, so I 'took' with me a piece of Salisbury that is part of the intellectual, moral and physical landscape for those who work, or live within, or come to visit the Cathedral Close. I took with me Elisabeth Frink's *Walking Madonna*. I began my sermon thus:

'As I walk from my house in the Close to the cathedral each day, I pass a woman of determined aspect, striding out from the cathedral towards the city; she looks straight ahead with single-minded purpose; she greets no-one on the way. I do not try to greet her either, or smile at her, but in my heart I acknowledge her, and all she stands for, as I move into God's holy house, where my soul, I pray, may magnify the Lord.

The woman is the *Walking Madonna*, a larger than life-size figure in bronze made by the great British sculptor, Elisabeth Frink. There she stands in her determined stride, in all weathers, sometimes holding the hand of a Japanese child posing for a picture; sometimes adorned by a garland, or holding a bunch of wild flowers, as the wondering, wandering public find a human shape in all the mass of mediaeval masonry and glass, with whom they can empathise and identify and understand.

And yet for all her humanity, the *Walking Madonna* is a disconcerting figure. Not only does she speak of singleness of purpose, not only does her gaunt frame speak of a spare idealism, not only does she proclaim an integrity and a truthfulness as all great art must -

all of which is disconcerting to our modern collusions and compromises. But she is walking away. The *Walking Madonna* walks away from the cathedral which bears her name, built to enshrine the gospel verities her life proclaimed. She walks away from shrine and altar, and liturgies of infinite beauty; away from the shimmer of silver and candlelight, and the pieties and platitudes of parsons and preachers; away from the green sward of quintessential English loveliness, and the elitism and privilege and comfortable living that surround it. She turns her back on the well-polished route to God, as though determined to seek him and find him out there in the city of noise and clamour and in the struggle to survive, where relationships are made and broken, where laughter and love and human goodness are joyfully celebrated right on the edges of living in the pain and squalor and meanness of life. The *Walking Madonna* walks away from the shrine, as though she is searching still for some out-house in which to bring forth God's word, and some hill outside the city wall where alone God's great work of redemption may be achieved.'

I quote the sermon at length, because that one female figure, who stands as a unique departure in the Frink corpus, nevertheless points to characteristics that can be identified with Elisabeth Frink's work as a whole. 'Spare idealism', 'integrity', 'truthfulness', are words one could use about much of Frink's work, and though not all her figures are walking, they all have energy and movement and vitality about them, created both by their spatial conception, and also by the characteristic Frink finish, which offers a rough-edged reflective surface which has not been mortiferously smoothed away. And then there is the intellectual and moral challenge which the *Walking Madonna* and much else in Elisabeth Frink's work provide. This isn't the only piece that disconcerts our comfortable ideas about what it is to be human, that reasserts idealism in an age of collusion and compromise; that reveals the human animal as well as human vulnerability, in an age which, though technologically sophisticated, remains emotionally and morally stunted; that develops an interior world of depth and simplicity and composure, even though the physical energy of so many of her works is what immediately arrests one.

When I was asked to write this article, I wanted to write about the spiritual understanding expressed in Elisabeth Frink's work. It was supposed that I would therefore want to concentrate on the pieces with religious implication - the *Walking Madonna*, *Risen Christ*, *Judas* - as though spiritual articulation were somehow confined to work inspired by explicitly religious themes. Such a context may indeed provide a clue to interpretation and sometimes challenge the traditional pre-suppositions and interpretations of religious sensibility. The *Walking Madonna* is a case in point. More traditional representations of the Madonna are demure, seated, passive, obedient - none of these adjectives can be said to apply to Frink's *Madonna*, as she strides purposefully from the Close. No doubt the title 'Madonna' and her location in the shadow of one of the world's great religious shrines, helps to establish the context for interpretation and perception. But would the work have been less spiritually charged if it had been 'Walking Woman' and placed outside the city library? And would the *Risen Christ*, which owes so much to the great giant heads of Frink's earlier work, have been less powerful in a spiritual sense if it had not borne that particular title, and had not been placed so conspicuously above the west door of Liverpool Cathedral?

It was DH Lawrence who expressed his sense of the sanctity of art and the religious sense that inspires all serious art:

'One needs something to make one's mood deep and sincere; there are so many little frets that prevent our coming to the real naked essence of our vision. I often think one ought to be able to pray before one works, and then leave it to the Lord. Isn't it always hard work to come to real grips with one's imagination, throw everything overboard? I feel as if I stood naked for the fire of Almighty God to go through me, and it's rather an awful feeling. One has to be so terribly religious to be an artist. I often think of my dear St Lawrence on his gridiron: he said "turn me over, brothers, I'm done enough on this side".'

Letter to Ernest Collings 1913

Edward Lucie-Smith points out that Elisabeth Frink was brought up as a Catholic, as though to explain why she should at the end of her life have returned to an explicitly religious theme (in creating the *Risen Christ* for Liverpool Cathedral). But what makes an artist's work interesting to a religious sensibility is not so much its explicit religiosity, as in the work's capacity to perceive, feel and express the pain and joy of the human condition. The spiritual value lies in the truthfulness and the compassion with which the artist articulates what he or she sees and feels. The beauty and economy of the articulation are the means by which the truth and the compassion are communicated to others. And so with Elisabeth Frink.

Her giants and her warriors are massive and animal-like, and strong and exuberant in their manhood. But they are not idealised heroes, and their nudity makes them accessible and vulnerable. Paradoxically, their very physicality and power, and seeming permanence, suggest a sense of the transience of all things. And while Elisabeth Frink's works suggest movement and physical strength and action, there is also an interior, almost contemplative quality, about them. They are composed, perfectly collected and recollected; their massiveness and energy is counter-poised by an interior quality, and the beholder is drawn on an inward journey. The *Green Man*, the *Easter Heads*, and the walking and standing men, and above all the head of *Christ*, all have this contemplative poise.

Then finally there is the work called *Judas*. Where for this exhibition could one place him in relation to the cathedral - the archetypal traitor, whose name has become a by-word for treachery? The decision was made to place him unambiguously where visitors enter and leave the cathedral, for Judas, though understandably vilified in the Gospels (especially that of John) and in Christian tradition, is one of the more interesting, paradoxical and psychologically complex characters who appears in the biblical narrative. For he was a friend, as well as a betrayer; a disciple as well as a deserter; a zealot as well as a plotter, and in modern spiritual readings, Judas needs to be rehabilitated on the map of spiritual discourse. For he represents the anguish, the cruel decisions that have to be made and lived with, the betrayals and collusions of which our century has witnessed more than most. Judas is a contemporary figure, not to be ignored by those who pass by. Elisabeth Frink's *Judas*, with its blindfolded face, recognises the anguish of the human predicament. The blindfold represents the purblindness of our human condition; it represents the incapacity

of humankind to bear the scrutiny of God - 'Ah, my dear, I cannot look on thee', and it recalls the terrible remorse of Judas' self-destruction.

The struggle of our humanity to be human in the face of all attempts to de-humanise and diminish, is expressed in the work of Elisabeth Frink. She disturbs our complacency, but also helps us to re-shape the moral and intellectual contours of our end-of-millennium landscape.

Jeremy Davies

Precentor, Salisbury Cathedral

Judas, 1963 (detail)

Elisabeth Frink

by Edward Lucie-Smith

'What I think I'm doing is creating my own myths - I'm not the slightest bit interested in other people's myths'.

Elisabeth Frink received many honours in her lifetime, but never a retrospective exhibition which corresponded to what she had in her mind's eye as a perfect setting for her work. She wanted the open air, ancient buildings, a sense that her sculptures were being allowed to live their own lives amidst the human lives surrounding them.

This exhibition, alas posthumous, provides the conditions she wanted. It will also, I think, give spectators a new vision of Frink's work - one much closer to her own personal conception of it.

Frink grew up during World War II, and spent part of her adolescence in a house near the great wartime bomber bases in Suffolk. The war in the air undoubtedly made a great impression on her - I was recently shown a very early sketchbook with sketches of aeroplanes, some of them on fire. These years provided some of the inspiration, but not the only inspiration, as she was always careful to point out, for her early sculptures of birds and birdmen.

Immediately after the war, when travel was still difficult, she was lucky enough to be taken to Venice by her family. The great works of art she saw there were catalysts which made their presence felt at just the right moment, when her imagination had already been excited by things she had seen illustrated in art books. She belonged in fact to the first generation of artists to be affected by the availability of these lavishly illustrated books, which had never been possible before. Yet books alone were not decisive: it was the direct experience of great artworks in their setting - for example, the looming presence of Verrocchio's equestrian statue of the condottiere *Bartolommeo Colleoni* beside the church of SS Giovanni e Paolo in Venice - which was decisive for her development.

Frink working on *Dying King*, 1962

seated on the *Canterbury Tales*,
illustrated with her etchings
(*Goggle Head* etchings behind),
early 1970s

She achieved success very swiftly as a sculptor, and in the 1950s became identified with a group of artists - Lynn Chadwick, Kenneth Armitage, Reg Butler - all of whom were much older than herself. Her first solo exhibition in London took place in 1952, and one of the works in it was purchased by the Tate Gallery.

This early recognition was a great piece of good fortune, as it allowed her to establish herself as an independent artist. From this period onwards she was never completely out of the public eye. The fact that she was a strikingly attractive woman, with a warm and open personality, reinforced her growing celebrity. It is interesting, and also symptomatic, that Frink never felt that she had been in any way disadvantaged by her gender. As a result, she had little sympathy with the feminist theories which, at a later date, sometimes attached themselves to her work.

On the other hand, Frink also tended to find herself typecast as a British figurative sculptor of largely local interest, whose work existed in isolation from what was taking place in Europe and the United States. This is an overly simplistic view which needs to be challenged. It is possible, for example, to draw direct comparisons with some of her European contemporaries, especially the French sculptor Germaine Richier, whose work Frink admired. She was also aware of a link between her own work and that of Giacometti, while at the same time being aware that their sculpture was at first glance unalike. The resemblance, she thought, was chiefly technical: 'In my early work I was... influenced by the way he built things up in plaster.'

What is perhaps more significant in the long term is Frink's position as a kind of premature neo-Expressionist - a forerunner of things which were to happen in German, Italian and some sections of American art from the late 1960s onward. It was her misfortune that this movement or group of movements - the Germans, Italians and Americans were in fact different from one another - only attracted attention in Britain rather late, at the beginning of the 1980s. Until then, the attention of the British avant-garde had been focused for two decades on abstraction - especially versions of Minimalism - and on Pop Art. It is evident that her work is widely divorced from either of these currents, and her feeling of alienation was the primary reason why she spent part of the 1960s and 1970s in France. However, she knew from the beginning that this self-exile would never be permanent, as her sensibility as an artist was too deeply rooted in the English tradition. Though she lived and worked in France for nearly a decade she took no part in artistic life there, and was not represented by any Parisian gallery.

In what sense was Frink Expressionist? Basically, because she regarded form as being primarily the outward manifestation of feeling:

'The reason why I sculpt dogs and horses is nothing to do with whether it's a foxhound or a bulldog or whatever. It's just a dog, and dogs tend to bring certain ideas to my mind... In the same way the horses are nothing to do with the horses you see here in England - the hunter, the show horse, the race horse. They're much more to do with the ancient spirit of the horse and its evolution in relation to man.'

Her sculptures are always concerned with a search for archetypes. It is significant in this respect that she recognised the importance of dreams in the evolution of her work, though she never worked from this dream material directly. Nevertheless their relationship to her sculpture was often clear: 'I had one the other day' she once told me, 'in which I was standing somewhere and huge bird shapes would roar past, soar up beside me until the sky was full of them'.

Lis was something of an insomniac, and consequently read a great deal. It was imaginative works which appealed to her in particular. She liked the work of the great Australian novelist Patrick White, and also that of leading Latin American writers: Gabriel Garcia Marquez, Carlos Fuentes, Mario Vargas Llosa. 'I'm much more interested in fantasy, something strange really, than I am in biography.'

Her view of her own creative process was quite clear:

'What I think I'm doing is creating my own myths - I'm not the slightest bit interested in other people's myths. To look at, yes, but not as sources for my own work. For example, I'm not interested in the Greek myths. I don't want to use them as an inspiration for what I do. I might do images of flight, but they're nothing to do with Icarus... None of my things are to do with ancient myths, with the possible exception of the *Green Man*. I just work out of my head.'

One image which was especially important to Frink was that of the human head itself. She attempted it over and over again, usually preferring to work in series. The large *Desert Quartet*, for example, were inspired by the feeling she got when she visited the desert in Tunisia, whereas the earlier *Goggle Heads* embody feelings about tyranny, and specifically about the Algerian War and its aftermath. Their starting point was a newspaper photograph of the sinister General Oufkir, at one time head of the Algerian secret police:

'Heads have always been very important to me as vehicles for sculpture. A head is infinitely variable. It's complicated and it's extremely emotional. Everyone's emotions are in their faces. It's not surprising that there are sculptures of massive heads going way back, or that lots of other artists beside myself have found the subject fascinating.'

Frink's first marriage had been to a Frenchman whose family was domiciled in Ireland. She found Ireland enormously fascinating and sympathetic. Through her visits there she became familiar with early Celtic iconography, and in particular with the ancient Celtic cult of the head, represented in museums by a number of primitive stone sculptures. The severed head, for the pagan Celts, was often endowed with oracular powers - an idea very likely to appeal to Frink's temperament, and one which seems to have left a lasting residue in her work.

Another image to which she returned again and again in the course of her career was that of the nude male body - the embodiment of the warrior or hero. She was always extremely definite that female bodies had no appeal to her from a sculptural point of view, and she was also hostile to the idea of drapery. For these two reasons the *Walking Madonna* in Salisbury, one of the most familiar of her images to the general public, simply because of its site, is also an exception in her output.

The reason for the success of the piece, despite the difficulties it caused her, is that it very successfully embodies a simple idea - that of the grieving mother - and therefore strikes the spectator with much greater emotional force than we are accustomed to finding in most contemporary sculptures. Frink, though not interested in the outward forms of religion, nevertheless thought of herself as a believing Christian:

'I think that being Christian is a matter of believing in another power, believing in God. I believe in the survival of the spirit, and of the soul. The spirit of people lives on, and is always there.'

It is undoubtedly this belief that gives her religious sculptures so much force. The *Madonna* in Salisbury is matched by her final work, the gigantic *Risen Christ* for the Anglican cathedral in Liverpool.

In addition to thinking of herself as Christian, Frink was strongly humanitarian, which does not always amount to the same thing. One of her criticisms of Catholicism, the faith in which she had been brought up, was its inability to tackle problems of poverty and over-population, especially in Latin America, where some of the most cherished Catholic doctrines seemed to her designed to make matters worse rather than better.

How are we to place Frink's achievement within the context both of art in Britain and twentieth century art? As is well known, Britain is not historically celebrated for its sculptures. In the late eighteenth century John Flaxman made himself into an international name, but this was thanks to his outline engravings illustrating classical texts, rather than his three-dimensional work. After that there was an hiatus until the appearance of Henry Moore. Frink is not as well known as Moore in international terms, nor indeed is she as renowned as Sir Anthony Caro or some of Caro's followers and successors. Here in Britain, however, she enjoyed and continues to enjoy a unique position, as a sculptor whose work communicates directly with the public, without the need for too much critical exegesis. It seems likely that this reputation will continue to grow. Indeed, if the prices given at auction for her work are any guide, her reputation has risen steadily since her death.

Where the international scene is concerned, recognition depends on two factors. First, on the realisation that she is not isolated, a quirky product of an equally quirky culture, perpetually out of step with what is taking place both in continental Europe and the United States, but part of a broad Expressionist current which flows through a great deal of twentieth century art. Second, on the survival of the kind of sculpture she herself practised. Keenly interested in all new developments in art, Frink was well aware of the new conceptual and environmental experiments which now play so large a part in the great international exhibitions, such as the Kassel Documenta. She nevertheless remained firmly convinced of the centrality of what she herself did, which was to make objects in time-resistant materials which would animate and give meaning to any context in which they were placed. The fact that these objects were figurative increased their power and multiplied the number of meanings which could be attached to them.

Edward Lucie-Smith

Author and Art Critic
co-author with the artist of *Frink: A Portrait*,
Bloomsbury, London, 1994.
All quotations are taken from the book.

with one of the *Tributes*, late 1970s

A certain unexpectedness

'One thing I'd like would be to have a large retrospective one day, somewhere outside. What I see in my mind's eye is somewhere where there's a lot of stone - ancient buildings. I'd like to see my work in an architectural setting ... a place where people walk, and go about their daily business. So that's the ideal I now have for a big show of mine. I love the thought of people just walking by and thinking, "Oh, there's something over there, something watching." Your sculpture is in the midst of life, but still has a certain unexpectedness - that's a nice relationship.'[1]

Elisabeth Frink's *Walking Madonna* - a gaunt purposeful striding figure is a familiar landmark in Salisbury's Cathedral Close. At times the sculpture disappears amongst the crowds of visitors, then re-emerges as a solitary figure dwarfed by the grey bulk of Cathedral walls and towering spire. The *Madonna* confounds expectations of maternal stereotypes. The initial controversy that arose at her arrival in 1981 still erupts from time to time. The figure presents a paradox: she permanently confers a sense of human scale to the Cathedral and its Close and yet the human qualities expressed by the sculpture challenge assumptions, provoking contradictory responses of both affection and hostility.

This exhibition at Salisbury developed from the presence of Frink's *Walking Madonna* in the Cathedral Close and the proximity of the town to Woolland, her final home and work place. The aim of the exhibition was to bring together a significant number of Frink's sculptures and graphic works and to place them into an everyday setting as she had desired.

Locating the sculptures in and around Salisbury Cathedral has involved numerous considerations. The humanist qualities of pieces such as the heads and male figures presented many challenges when siting them in a place of worship; even the obviously religious works such as *Christ* and the maquette for *Risen Christ* raised a number of issues. Furthermore, Salisbury Cathedral, a collective focus for spiritual and theological ideas and experiences, is also a place of work, a tourist attraction and then, during the Festival, a site for performances. The scale of the building, the internal mixture of styles and imagery and the bustle of people affects the spectators' perspective of the sculptures and yet the spiritual nature of the environment adds its own resonance to the works.

For example, *Judas* was placed just outside the North Porch, symbolically at the threshold of the Cathedral, representing the theological discourses relating to his position within the church.

The core of Frink's work is figurative. She saw her sculptures as 'places to put an idea or feeling'[2] and despite early and continued acclaim many British art institutions were nervous of her work. 'Critics and other sculptors have long recognised that Elisabeth Frink is a sculptor of rare gift and seriousness. She is outstanding in her generation. We are also inclined to hedge nevertheless about the work she happens to be doing at any particular moment.'[3]

Elisabeth Frink's sculptures are often positioned by art critics in the shadow of mainstream twentieth century art movements. She was one of the few outstanding sculptors of her post-war generation not to move into abstraction. 'I'm a slow developer, a very unfashionable thing nowadays when everyone seems to feed chiefly on novelty, in particular the critics and public galleries. My ideas come to me naturally, no blinding inspirations. I am more instinctive as an artist, than intellectual. Because my next piece may resemble my last, perhaps there's a feeling I'm no longer in the vanguard, whatever that may be. Certainly I sometimes feel isolated, alone in my style of representing what I care about. But I'm grateful: my public sales are always good.'[4]

Frink was not conventionally progressive, she was not interested in experiment for its own sake. She was, however, influenced by contemporary issues and events and by evolving and developing her responses to these, her sculptures often present a disquieting commentary on modern times and can be unexpectedly innovative. She used images as a shell for feelings, for realistic representations

were not her concern. She was often reluctant to discuss her work and had a fine disregard for words, 'I'd like you to publish only pictures - who on earth wants to read about sculpture.'[5] But in a series of discussions with Edward Lucie-Smith, held during the last stages of her fight against cancer, she talked extensively about her work describing it as 'the combination of something past, the Celtic element, something now and something which might possibly be in the future.'[6] The sculptures of Elisabeth Frink contain a limited and recurring range of shapes: man, heads, certain animal and bird forms; through these she expressed her evolving preoccupations. She pushed against the boundaries of tradition rather than relegating them to the scrap-heap: 'My main sources have been quite precise, but they turned into something en-route. There's an accumulation of ideas.'[7]

The sculptures and graphic works chosen for this exhibition illustrate Frink's interpretation of contemporary issues and artistic concerns. Rather than charting progressive differences in her style it was decided to display examples of her work which illustrate how particular themes recur and are inherent in her sculptures. Although Frink used familiar human and animal forms, there was no concession to romantic feelings. She conveyed her ideas in almost abstract terms through her sculptural rendering of movement, tension, form and latterly, colour.

Her early work was full of implicit threat and aggression: 'Early observation, in the country, of living and dead forms is the foundation for a great deal of my work. Violence in a dead form is quite different, the actual forms that dead things take... I am very well aware of violence in the world... I am interested that men and animals are confronted by combat in their lives, some sort of menace, and must defend themselves... I try to create the stress and tension this causes.'[8] The-post war preoccupation of British artists with aggression and menace which manifested itself in discordant sculptural forms are evident in her early works such as *Warrior Bird*, *Dead Hen* and *Warrior*, with their rough and craggy expressionistic surfaces. Her later series of *Soldiers' Heads* and *Goggle Heads* still express malice, no longer through rough and spiky forms, but are threatening and threatened at the same time by a simplification of form, a reliance on bulk and smoothness of texture suggesting dominance and thuggish power. The reflective goggles not only hide the eyes of the oppressor but act as mirrors to the spectator.

Frink's absorption with 'ideas of the head' explored early in her career through semi-abstract works such as *Plant Head*, *Fish Head* and *Carapace* were crystallised as a vehicle for her humanist concerns. The *Tributes* and *Prisoner's Head* were a direct response to human rights issues which she keenly championed. She wrote of Amin in 1977, 'It is a disgrace that the governments of the free-world, including our own are just sitting on the fence. They are doing nothing to help save lives in Uganda and nothing to stop this monstrous man from continuing to massacre thousands more. They should unite and it should be the obsession of every free human being to see that some organization is formed to intervene and stop the massacre... These days 'diplomacy' rates higher than human life.'[9] Her sculptured heads grew bigger and more monumental. The dynamic impact of the pieces were emphasised by the textural treatment of the bronze surfaces. The irregular gouges of *In memoriam* became transformed into a rhythmic pattern of incisions covering the surface of the *Desert Quartet*. The cumulative repetition of identical heads in the *Desert Quartet* reinforced by the repetitive regularity of surface notches, provides coherence and

strength to the group and at the same time introduces a sense of disquiet and menace, which is enhanced by the white patinated bronze surface.

Latent energy and movement dominate her work. Figures in space and spinning, falling men were the forerunners of a long sequence of sculptures in which she explored her fascination with movement; implicitly expressed as action or implied by contained restlessness. She developed this theme in a wide range of strong sensuous forms: *Falling Man* through to *Running Man* and eventually *Seated Man*. In pieces such as *Horse* and *Large Rolling Horse* movement is obvious, but in *Leonardo's Dog* or *Chinese Horse* our interest is concentrated on static qualities, such as coiled tension, equilibrium and volume. In some works we are confronted by the concurrence of movement and motionless; *Homme Libellule* (dragon-fly man), and *Sleeping Horse* amongst many.

The metamorphic figures including *Birdman* and *Winged Figure* were early expressions of her interest in man and animal relationships. Sculptures such as *Horse and Rider* and the later *Horseman* illustrate how the archetypal image of man and horse were continually re-defined by Frink, each serving as a vehicle for an exploration of different creative ideas: 'I am quite interested in horses, not obsessed with them in a social sense, but interested in the form that they embody, in their wild state and their relationship with man, which is much more interesting than just doing a horse.'[10]

Colour was to become a crucial component of many of her later works; including *Easter Head* and *Green Man*. 'I don't want to do brown bronzes any more, the way the Victorians did them. I want to use more brilliant hues.'[11] When she first started to experiment

drawing in the studio at Woolland, mid 1980s

24

with colour she painted the bronzes, but she found the flat, even quality of the paint unsatisfactory. She also tried coloured glazes, which again were unsuccessful. Soon, with the assistance of her bronze-founder she was using chemicals to patinate the surface of the bronze, 'You heat the bronze up with a gas torch, then, when its really sizzling hot, you slosh on the chemicals till the bronze changes colour. It's magic.'[12] She was interested not just in the colours that could be achieved but also in the element of chance, building it into the creative process. The *Riace* figures with their colour-patinated faces continued Frink's exploration of familiar themes, 'I was fascinated by the fact that the figures have these two sides to them... I used different coloured patinas to put masks on the figures. It's a way of showing that their beauty in a sense hides what they are up to... The idea is that something might be bursting out of these people. They're restraining or constraining vessels of skin and muscle and sinew.'[13]

Throughout her working life Elisabeth Frink also explored her ideas and feelings through drawing and print-making. Unlike many other sculptors, Frink did not work from models. 'All my drawings are ideas which might lead up to sculpture, but they don't necessarily do so. The process is very important because it's a way of getting my ideas out on paper. But I've always liked drawing on a big scale... What I do is to make a group of drawings, working up to the very edge of the paper, then I put them aside for a while in order to think about them.'[14] Embryonic ideas were put down on paper with great vigour and sureness and there is a tactile quality to most of her graphic works. As with her sculptures, many images are drawn over and over again, but each is charged with spontaneity.

The power and beauty of Elisabeth Frink's sculptures originate in her ability to confound expectations and to create from archetypes a fresh vision. Her brilliance lies precisely in the unexpected characteristics of her work. 'I think what I'm doing is trying to set up a kind of encounter with the spectator, a dialogue between my sculptures and the public. People have to add part of themselves to make it work; they have to look into it as well as at it.'[15]

Annette Downing

Curator, Edwin Young Trust,
Wiltshire County Council and Salisbury Festival

1   E Lucie-Smith and E Frink,
    Frink A Portrait,
    Bloomsbury, London, 1994, p137
2   E Lucie-Smith and E Frink,
    Frink A Portrait, p125
3   F Laws, *Guardian,* 11.12.65, p6
4   G Hughes, *Arts Review,*
    June 1981, p229
5   G Hughes, *Arts Review,* p229
6   *Frink A Portrait,* p123
7   *Frink A Portrait,* p123
8   H Wheldon, *Monitor,* BBC,
    L Lee and E Frink,
    Macdonald & Co, 1962, p27
9   E Frink, *The Times,* 17.3.77, letters
10 E Frink, *The Times,* 3.12.76
11 *Frink A Portrait,* p54
12 *Frink A Portrait,* p57
13 *Frink A Portrait,* p126
14 *Frink A Portrait,* p134
15 *Frink A Portrait,* p64

Man and the animal world

As is the case with any artist of calibre whose working life has spanned four decades, it would be possible to mount almost any number of Elisabeth Frink exhibitions, each with its own focus or emphasis: Frink's work in the context of post-war figuration, Frink as portraitist, as printmaker, as sculptor of animals, as protagonist of human rights, Frink's use of colour in sculpture, etc., etc.. For this exhibition, almost all of the work has been chosen from the collection of Frink's son, Lin Jammet, who has been generously supportive from the beginning. Although the pieces chosen were made over a period of about thirty years, from 1958-1990, I have not tried to make this an even-handed retrospective by including an example of each of her many areas of interest. Instead, I've concentrated on the theme of Man and Man's relation to the animal world.

There must be no politically correct squeamishness about applying the word 'Man' here. Virtually all Frink's figure sculptures are of men and she had as robust, commonsense an attitude to maleness as she did towards animals. She loved men, she understood both their strengths and weaknesses and she had a particular genius at interpreting maleness in all its aspects, from the brutal to the tragic; always with dignity. Animals received the same even-handedness of vision. She could suggest their vulnerability and beauty as well as their menace and was particularly successful at depicting them simply 'being themselves'. She was good at this because she understood them so completely and kept a clear eye.

Sculptures such as *Leonardo's Dog* and the *Standing Horse* of 1982 are examples of this depiction of dog-ness and horse-ness. Their simplicity of means is deceptive, concealing profound understanding coupled with technical mastery. Frink's work of the 1950s and

early 1960s contains many images of disequilibrium or menace, no doubt part of her response to the moral and sculptural climate of that time. Several examples are included, most notably the sinister *Harbinger Bird* of 1961. It is interesting how many of her animal drawings and watercolours of that period show dead or wounded creatures, possibly images made of game destined for the pot. In her later work, grace and nobility are emphasised, especially in the images of horses. Where these are wounded or terrified, one realises that this is part of a crying out on the part of the sculpture against cruelty and inhumanity.

If red, the colour of blood, was among the first colours to enter Frink's graphic work, it was only one of the constituent colour-parts that began to play an important role in her sculpture after about 1985. For me, this introduction of colour, which was not achieved without a lengthy struggle, was one of Elisabeth Frink's most original and courageous inventions. Instead of contenting herself with doing what came naturally, so to speak, she pushed her work into another dimension in psychological terms and received little acclaim for having done so. I regret that it hasn't been poss-ible to include any coloured bronzes in this exhibition, but the *Seated Man* of 1986, which is really its centre-piece, would not have come to possess the gravitas he has without those experiments with colour. They changed everything. What we do have are two of the *Cut-out Running Man* series of 1988 which formed part of that early experimentation. Their wildness is both exhilarating and slightly unnerving.

I have also included two of the large gouaches of 1990 of *Baboon and Man*. This image, which Frink intended to extend into one or more large sculptures, is extraordinarily moving, as the male figure far from dominating the baboon, gazes up at him almost imploring-ly, as if seeking some lost wisdom. Illness and then death denied her that chance and we are the losers, as I feel certain that they (or even 'it') would have been among her finest achievements. As it is, she summoned enough strength to complete the *Risen Christ* for Liverpool and for that we must be grateful.

As I wrote above, *Seated Man* is the centre-piece of this exhibition, an image of quiet strength poised for action. Around him are grouped various animals, all central to the life of humankind: the patient dog, horses both for sport and work, water buffaloes like-wise, the boar for food (as well as his essential unapproachability), and birds for the air and the table. Most of these are familiar com-panions or ancient objects of the chase. There is, however, one dog howling with some mysterious, lonely secret and a baboon who looks about to say, 'which of us came first?'. As well as these, we have two alter-egos, one the *Standing Man* of 1970 who has simply endured, the other the *Running Man* of eight years later, in which male athleticism is infused with coltish grace.

Besides the gouaches and watercolors already referred to, I have included a largish number of Frink's prints, both etchings and litho-graphs. I've done this not only because I greatly respect her as a printmaker but also because I think the making of prints sharpened and deepened her use of line and gave greater scope for her colour sense. Several drawings, such as *Man* and the beautiful *Man with Horse*, have never been exhibited before. Her prints of the Greek myths, shown here by a small selection, are among her most successful and inventive images, bringing together her gifts for expressing violence, calm, tragedy and humour.

Elisabeth Frink was a remarkable, wonderful woman with great instinctive understanding of human beings, as well as birds and animals and the ability, honed by years of observation and practise, to enable us to grasp their inter-connection. We rejoice at what she made and left for us.

John Hubbard

Painter

Leonardo's Dog in the garden at Woolland, early 1990s

In the studio, Woolland

'...a white, quiet place,
littered for action.
From here all that we
really know of Lis Frink
finally emerges.
It is the other world,
the kind of inside her
working mind. A scribble
of notes and images,
and the various bits
of homely junk, wire,
old newspapers,
firewood, which she
uses to build her figures.'

Laurie Lee

'I could not work without a place to work where I am able to shut myself off. I don't naturally or consciously draw any of my ideas or forms from the outside world. When I have left this studio I have left it... I like to create everything in here. This is the place where I work, I have to keep it apart from everything else.'

Elisabeth Frink

Working in plaster

'She doesn't hack, she builds. Carving, she says, is too slow for her, she has to work quickly while the idea is still with her.'

Laurie Lee

'I have a technique of building plaster of Paris up and carving which suits my way of working because I get my ideas very quickly, and like to see stuff go up fast.'

Elisabeth Frink

Building

Making an armature is really building up a skeleton in iron. Whether it's a large one or a small one it's all the same.

Modelling

I use chicken-wire, and hessian soaked in plaster, which gives a good surface to build on, and then I just pile more plaster on with my hands. I often use sawdust and stuff mixed up with the plaster, which gives a much more gritty texture. Then I correct as I go along.

Carving

Right from the beginning I carve it back. It's a constant process of rebuilding and adjusting, of carving back, until I've got just what I want.

31

Elisabeth Frink with *Dog* and *Riace* figures

Seated Man – an early experiment
with painted colour

at Woolland with Alex Csáky and
the *Cut-out Men* 1988 – which were
commissioned by Issey Miyake

Elisabeth Frink in her studio at Woolland

Dying King 1963
(CR103)

Running man 1978
(CR238)

opposite
Praecursor 1976
(CR231)

Seated Man II 1986
(SC20)

Lying Down and Standing Buffalo
1987/1988
(SC33/SC34)

First Horse 1990
(SC57)

Chinese Horse II (rolling) 1989
(SC45)

Dog, at the foundry 1992
SC73

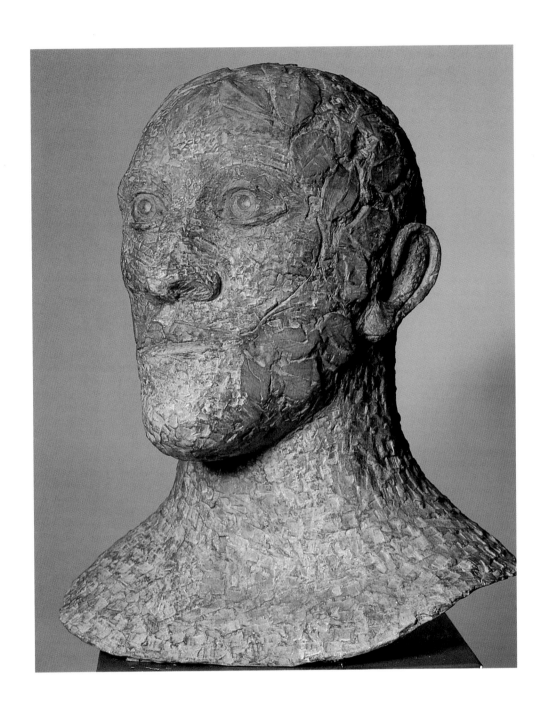

Green Man 1991
(SC65)

Easter Head 1 1989
(SC41)

opposite
Desert Quartet III 1989
(SC51)

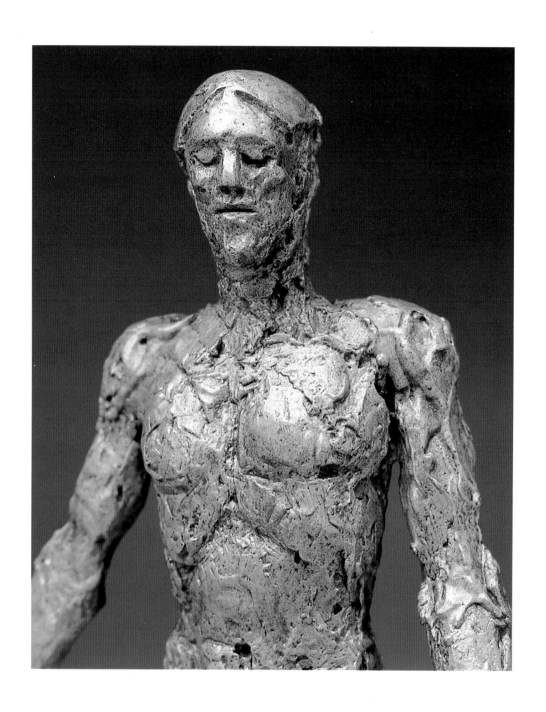

Maquette for *Risen Christ* 1992
(SC67)

Maquette for *Walking Madonna* 1981
(CR262)

Head of Christ 1983
(CR278)

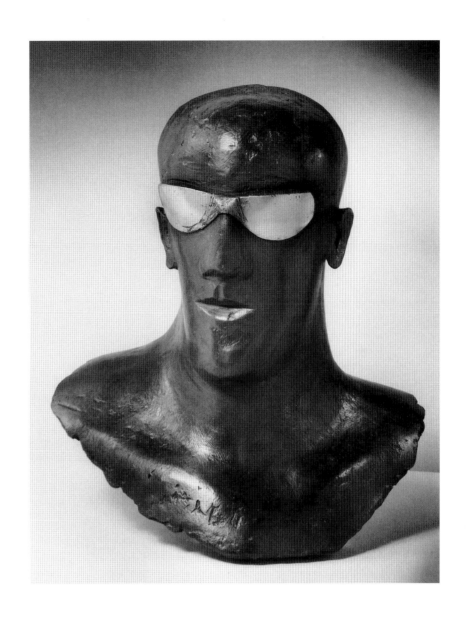

Goggle Head 1969
(CR183)

Head 1969
(CR184)

Horse's Head 1963
(CR95)

Dead Hen 1957
(CR32)

Warrior Bird 1953
(CR12)

Horizontal Birdman I 1962
(CR 89)

Horse and Rider 1970
(CR193)

Sleeping Horse 1972
(CR202)

Horse 1980
(CR256)

Large Rolling Over Horse 1975
(CR218)

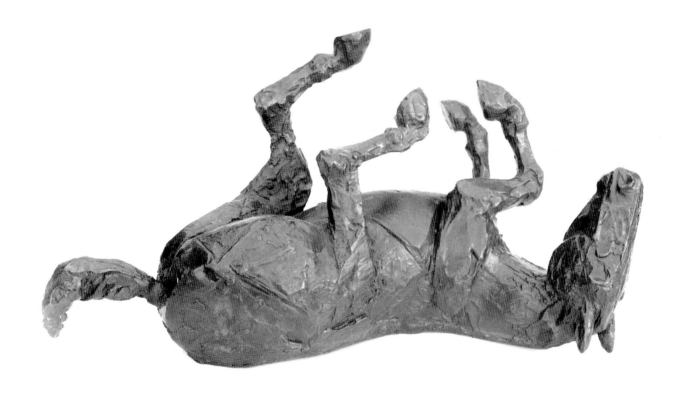

Large Rolling Horse 1985
(SC00)

Wild Boar 1975
(CR216)

Dog 1958
(CR46)

Selected biographical résumé

Frink with early *Seated Man*, plaster, 1951

1930	November 14, born in Thurlow, Suffolk, England
1947 - 49	Studied at Guildford School of Art
1949 - 53	Studied at Chelsea School of Art
1952	Tate Gallery purchased *Bird*
1953	Won prize in competition for *Monument to the unknown political prisoner*
1953 - 61	Taught at Chelsea School of Art
1955	Married Michel Jammet, one son Lin Jammet First solo exhibition at Waddington Galleries, London Solo exhibition at Bertha Schaefer Gallery, New York
1954 - 62	Taught at St Martin's School of Art
1957	First major public commissions for Harlow New Town - *Boar*, and Bethnal Green Borough Council - *Blind Beggar and Dog*
1964	Married Edward Pool
1965 - 67	Visiting Instructor at Royal College of Art
1967	Moved to France First exhibition in Dorset at the Hambledon Gallery, Blandford
1969	Awarded CBE
1971	Elected Associate of the Royal Academy
1973	Returned to England
1974	Married Alexander Csáky

1976	Moved to Dorset
1977	Elected Royal Academician
	Awarded her first Honorary Doctorate
	by University of Surrey
1980	First exhibition in Salisbury at Salisbury Arts Centre
1981	*Walking Madonna* bought for Salisbury Cathedral
	Appointed Trustee, Welsh Sculpture Trust
1982	Solo exhibition at Dorset County Museum,
	Dorchester
	Awarded DBE
	Awarded Doctorate by Royal College of Art
1983	Solo exhibition at Yorkshire Sculpture Park
1985	Solo exhibition at the Royal Academy of Arts,
	London
1985/86	Commission from the Dorset Natural
	History and Archaeological Society for the
	Memorial to the Dorset Martyrs, Dorchester
1989	Retired from the Board of Trustees of
	the British Museum
1990	Solo exhibition at the National Museum
	of Women in the Arts, Washington DC
1992	Awarded Companion of Honour
	Completed last major public commission -
	Risen Christ for West facade, Anglican
	Cathedral, Liverpool
1993	18 April - died of cancer

Selected further reading

R Berthoud, *Elisabeth Frink:
a comment on the future*
The Times, 3 December 1976

*Elisabeth Frink: Sculpture, Catalogue
Raisonné* Harpvale Books, Salisbury, 1984

E Frink, *Sculpture in parks*
The Times, 30 June 1976

H Griffin, *Elisabeth Frink*
Studio, October 1961

G Hughes, *Elisabeth Frink*
Arts Review, 5 June 1981

S Kent and H. Kramer, *Elisabeth Frink:
Sculpture and Watercolor 1964 -1979*
Massachusetts Review, Spring 1980

C Lilley, *Elisabeth Frink Memorial
Exhibition*, catalogue, Yorkshire Sculpture
Park, 1994

E Lucie-Smith, *Elisabeth Frink:
Sculpture since 1984 and Drawings*
Art Books International, London, 1994

E Lucie-Smith and E Frink,
Frink a portrait, Bloomsbury,
London, 1994

I McManus, *Elisabeth Frink:
An Open Air Retrospective,*
Arts Review, 2 September, 1983

R. Melville, *The art of being literal,*
Architectural Review, p349-352,
December 1972

E Mullins, *The Art of Elisabeth Frink,*
Lund Humphries, London, 1972

B Robertson, *Elisabeth Frink:
Open Air Retrospective*, catalogue introduction, Yorkshire Sculpture Park, 1983

B Robertson, *Elisabeth Frink: Sculpture
and Drawings*, catalogue, The National
Museum of Women in the Arts,
Washington DC, 1990

L Sabbath, *Sculptor prefers
Males as Models*, Gazette, Montreal,
11 November 1981

H Wheldon, *Monitor: An Anthology,
Elisabeth Frink*, p24, Macdonald & Co.,
London, 1962

An extensive bibliography can be found
in the Catalogue Raisonné.

List of works

CR and SC numbers refer to the catalogue numbers from the two volume catalogue raisonné of Elisabeth Frink's sculptures and drawings.

SFC
refers to works shown at Salisbury Cathedral

SFL
refers to works shown at Salisbury Library and Galleries

DCM
refers to works shown at Dorchester

1   *Warrior Bird* 1953 (CR12)
bronze
49.5cm
unique
SFL

2   *Warrior's Head* 1954 (CR23)
bronze
40.6cm
edition of 2
cast from *Warrior* 1954 (CR22)
SFC

3   *Dead Hen* 1957 (CR32)
bronze
16.5cm
edition of 6
SFL

4   *Dog* 1957 (CR38)
bronze
69.9cm
edition of 3 cast from
Blind Beggar and Dog
(CR37)
SFC

5   *Bird* 1958 (CR44)
bronze
50.2cm
edition of 10
DCM

6   *Dog* 1958 (CR46)
bronze
96.5 x 96.5cm
edition of 4
DCM

7   *Pietà* 1959 (CR53)
bronze
113.7 x 38.1cm
unique
SFC

8   *Crucifixion* 1959 (CR54)
bronze
113.7 x 38.1cm
unique
SFC

9   *Winged Figure* 1959 (CR55)
bronze
61cm
edition of 6
SFL

10   *Dormant Head* 1961 (CR68)
bronze
19.1cm
edition of 6
SFL

11   *Fish Head* 1961 (CR69)
bronze
19.7cm
edition of 6
SFL

12   *Sentinel I* 1961 (CR71)
bronze
129.5cm
edition of 6
SFL

13   *Falling Man* 1961 (CR72)
bronze
68.6cm
edition of 6
SFL

in the studio yard with *Judas* and *Dying King*, early 1960s

14 *Harbinger Bird III* 1961 (CR77)
bronze
43.2cm
edition of 9
SFL and DCM

15 *Horizontal Birdman I* 1962
(CR 89)
bronze
12.1 x 40.6cm
edition of 10
maquette for Alcock and Brown
memorial (CR91)
SFL

16 *Small Eagle* 1962 (CR92)
bronze
23.5cm
edition of 9
SFL

17 *Birdman* 1962 (CR93)
bronze
80cm
edition of 6
SFL

18 *Horse's Head* 1963 (CR95)
bronze
26.7 x 45.7cm
edition of 6
SFL

19 *Carapace I* 1963 (CR96)
bronze
26.7 x 31.8cm
edition of 6
SFL

20 *Plant Head* 1963 (CR98)
bronze
73.7cm
edition of 6
SFL

21 *Judas* 1963 (CR102)
bronze
190.5cm
edition of 3
SFC

22 *Dying King* 1963 (CR103)
bronze
90.2 x 198.1cm
edition of 3
SFC

23 *Winged Figures* 1964 (CR107)
bronze
44.5cm
edition of 7
SFL

24 *First Man* 1964 (CR113)
bronze
193cm
edition of 3
SFC

25 *Soldier's Head III* 1965 (CR119)
bronze
35.6cm
edition of 6
SFC

26 *Soldier's Head IV* 1965 (CR120)
bronze
35.6cm
edition of 6
SFC

27 *Homme Libellule II* 1965 (CR145)
bronze
38.1cm
edition of 7
SFL

28 *Head* 1967 (CR165)
bronze
53.3cm
edition of 6
SFC

29 *Head* 1967 (CR166)
bronze
44.5cm
edition of 6
SFC

30 *Head* 1967 (CR168)
bronze
50.8cm
edition of 6
SFC

31 *Boar* 1968 (CR172)
bronze
14 x 21cm
edition of 7
SFL

32 *Goggled Head I* 1969 (CR180)
bronze
61cm
edition of 6
SFC

33 *Goggled Head II* 1969 (CR181)
bronze
64.8cm
edition of 6
SFC

34 *Goggle Head* 1969 (CR182)
bronze
63.5cm
edition of 6
SFC

35 *Goggle Head* 1969 (CR183)
bronze
62.2cm
edition of 6
SFC

36 *Head* 1969 (CR184)
bronze
66cm
edition of 6
SFL

37 *Horse and Rider* 1969 (CR189)
bronze
31.8cm
edition of 7
SFL

38 *Horse and Rider* 1970 (CR193)
bronze
52.1 x 50.8cm
edition of 7
DCM

39 *Man* 1970 (CR195)
bronze
188cm
edition of 3
DCM

40 *Sleeping Horse* 1972 (CR202)
bronze
104.1 x 203.2cm
edition of 4
SFC

41 *Wild Boar* 1975 (CR216)
bronze
71.1 x 99.1cm
edition of 6
SFC and DCM

42 *Large Rolling Over Horse* 1975
(CR218)
bronze
38.1 x 52.1 x 30.5cm
edition of 6
DCM

43 *Tribute I* 1975 (CR219)
bronze
68.6cm
edition of 6
SFC

44 *Tribute II* 1975 (CR220)
bronze
69.9cm
edition of 6
SFC

45 *Tribute III* 1975 (CR221)
bronze
68.6cm
edition of 6
SFC

46 *Tribute IV* 1975 (CR222)
bronze
66cm
edition of 6
SFC

47 *Praecursor* 1976 (CR231)
bronze
215.9cm
edition of 3
SFC

48 *Running Man* 1978 (CR238)
bronze
193cm
edition of 3
SFC and DCM

49 *Horse* 1980 (CR256)
bronze
274.3 x 27.3cm
edition of 3
commissioned by the Earl
of March for Goodwood
Racecourse, Sussex
SFC

50 *Eagle Trophy* 1980 (CR260)
bronze
39.4cm
edition of 7
commissioned by The Royal
Philharmonic Society and
Performing Right Society for
the Leslie Boosey Award
SFL

51 *Lin Jammet* 1980
bronze
45cm
unique
SFL

52 *Madonna* 1981 (CR262)
bronze
30.2cm
edition of 8
maquette for *Walking Madonna*
(CR263)
SFL

53 *Walking Madonna* 1981 (CR263)
bronze
205.7cm
edition of 3
SFC

54 *Hands for Madonna* 1981
(CR264)
bronze
8.9 x 22.9cm and 8.9 x 28.6cm
editions of 6
cast from *Walking Madonna*
(CR263)
SFL

55 *In memoriam I* 1981 (CR265)
bronze
127cm
edition of 6
SFC

56 *In memoriam II* 1981 (CR266)
bronze
127cm
edition of 6
SFC

57 *Prisoner's Head* 1982 (SC36)
bronze
44.5cm
edition of 6
from *Man* (CR238)
SFC

58 *Standing Horse* 1982 (CR270)
bronze
50.8 x 58.4cm
edition of 6
DCM

59 *Rolling Horse* 1982 (CR273)
bronze
24.1 x 49.5cm
edition of 6
DCM

60 *Christ* 1983 (CR278)
bronze
77cm
edition of 6
commissioned for All Saints'
Church, Basingstoke
SFC

61 *Atlas* 1983 (SC0)
bronze
2.75m
unique
commissioned by
Commercial Union
SFC

62 *Horseman* 1984 (SC2)
bronze
81.3 x 81.3cm
edition of 6
SFL

63 *Large Rolling Horse* 1985 (SC00)
bronze
49.5 x 23cm
edition of 9
SFL

64 *Seated Man II* 1986 (SC20)
bronze
134.6 x 85 x 76.2cm
edition of 4
SFC and DCM

65   Riace I 1986 (SC16)
bronze
2.11m
edition of 4
commissioned for WH Smith
headquarters, Swindon, Wiltshire
SFC

66   Large Dog 1986 (SC23)
bronze
90.2 x 119.4cm
edition of 6
SFC

67   Riace II 1986 (SC28)
bronze
2.18m
edition of 4
SFC

68   Self Portrait 1987 (SC32)
bronze
45.75 x 30.5cm
edition of 6
SFL and DCM

69   Lying Down Buffalo 1987 (SC33)
bronze
87.6cm x 2.69m
edition of 2
commissioned by Hong Kong
Land Company for Exchange
Square, Hong Kong
SFC

70   Standing Buffalo 1988 (SC34)
bronze
1.47 x 2.97m
edition of 2
commissioned by Hong Kong
Land Company for Exchange
Square, Hong Kong
SFC

71   Maquette for Standing Buffalo
1988 (SC37b)
37 x 10 x 18cm
bronze
edition of 12
DCM

72   Lying Down Buffalo 1988 (SC38)
bronze
18.4 x 50.8cm
edition of 10
DCM

73   Riace III 1988 (SC42)
bronze
2.18m
edition of 4
SFC

74   Easter Head I 1989 (SC41)
bronze
49.5 x 50.8cm
edition of 6
SFC

75   Easter Head II 1989 (SC44)
bronze
50.8 x 45.75cm
edition of 6
SFC

76   Chinese Horse II (rolling) 1989
(SC45)
bronze
23.5 x 40.6cm
edition of 9
SFL

77   Chinese Horse III (standing) 1989
(SC47)
bronze
48.9 x 48.9cm
edition of 8
SFL

78   Riace IV 1989 (SC48)
bronze
2.21m
edition of 4
SFC

79   Desert Quartet I 1989 (SC49)
bronze
130.8 x 124.5 x 87.6cm
edition of 6
SFC

80   Desert Quartet II 1989 (SC50)
bronze
128 x 116.8 x 76.2cm
edition of 6
SFC

81   Desert Quartet III 1989 (SC51)
bronze
127 x 115.6 x 76.2cm
edition of 6
SFC

82   Desert Quartet IV 1989 (SC52)
bronze
122.5 x 109.25 x 80cm
edition of 6
SFC

83   Walking Baboon 1989 (SC54)
bronze
29.8 x 14.6 x 38.75cm
edition of 9
SFL

84   Seated Baboon 1989 (SC55)
bronze
37.5 x 25.4 x 40.6cm
edition of 9
SFL and DCM

85   First Horse 1990 (SC57)
bronze
57.1 x 57.1cm
edition of 6
DCM

86   Leonardo's Dog 1990 (SC58)
bronze
99.7 x 38.1 x 101.6cm
edition of 6
DCM

87   Green Man 1991 (SC65)
bronze
57.8 x 48.25 x 34.35cm
edition of 6
SFL

88   Leonardo's Dog II 1992 (SC66)
bronze
101.6 x 44.5 x 87.6cm
edition of 6
SFL

89   Maquette for Risen Christ 1992 (SC67)
bronze
26.7 x 15.2 x 53.3cm
edition of 12
SFC

90   Dog 1992 (SC73)
bronze
22.9 x 17.8cm
sold in aid of the Hospital for
Sick Children, Great Ormond
Street, London
SFL

91 *Reclining Horse* 1974
    tapestry, wool
    1.8 x 2.55m
    edition of 25
    commissioned by Barry Cronan
    Fine Art Ltd., hand knotted
    by Raj Dutt, India
    SFC

92 *On the road to Chartres*
    circa 1980
    tapestry, wool
    1.85 x 2.75m
    edition of 25
    commissioned by Barry Cronan
    Fine Art Ltd., hand knotted
    by Raj Dutt, India
    SFC

93 *Cut-out Man I* 1988
    painted hardboard
    unique
    commissioned by Issey Miyake
    SFL

94 *Cut-out Running Man II* 1988
    painted hardboard
    unique
    commissioned by Issey Miyake
    DCM

95 *Cut-out Running Man III* 1988
    painted hardboard
    unique
    commissioned by Issey Miyake
    DCM

96 *Cut-out Man IV* 1988
    painted hardboard
    unique
    commissioned by Issey Miyake
    SFL

97 *Two Men with knives* 1955
    ink
    70 x 60cm
    SFL

98 *Falling Man* 1958
    watercolour
    74.7 x 55cm
    SFL

99 *Cuchulain* 1959
    watercolour
    76.5 x 56cm
    SFL

100 *Predatory Bird* 1961
     chalk
     72.3 x 54cm
     DCM

101 *Untitled* (winged beast) 1963
     watercolour
     76.5 x 56.5cm
     SFL

102 *Plant Head* 1964
     charcoal
     76.3 x 56cm
     SFL

103 *Dead Pheasant* 1965
     watercolour
     73.5 x 54cm
     DCM

104 *Spinning Man* 1965
     lithograph
     Curwen Chilford Prints
     80.5 x 58cm
     SFL

105 *Soldier's Head* 1965
     watercolour
     76.2 x 56cm
     SFL

106 *Head* circa 1965
     watercolour and pencil
     76.8 x 56.5cm
     SFL

107 *Oufkir* 1966
     watercolour and charcoal
     76.2 x 56.2cm
     SFL

108 *Dead Hare* 1967
     watercolour
     73 x 54cm
     DCM

109 *Boar* 1967
     watercolour and pencil
     74.2 x 56cm
     SFL

110 *Osprey with fish* circa 1968
     coloured etching
     51.5 x 44cm
     DCM

111 *Owl* circa 1968
     coloured etching
     51.5 x 44cm
     DCM

112 *Two Vultures* circa 1968
     coloured etching
     51.5 x 44cm
     DCM

113 *Goshawk* circa 1968
     coloured etching
     51.5 x 44cm
     DCM

114 *Bull* circa 1968
     lithograph
     Curwen Chilford Prints
     77.6 x 59.3cm
     SFL

115 *Lion* 1968
     watercolour and pencil
     100 x 70cm
     SFL

116 *Man with horse* 1971
     watercolour and pencil
     73.5 x 98cm
     DCM

117 *Man and Horse V* 1971
     lithograph
     60 x 80cm
     SFL

118 *The Prologue* 1972
     from *The Canterbury Tales*
     etching
     80 x 60cm
     SFL

119 *Horse and Oyster-catcher* 1974
     watercolour and pencil
     29.5 x 40.8cm
     SFL

120 from *The Odyssey* circa 1974
     coloured etching
     55 x 36.8cm
     DCM

121 *Odysseus* circa 1974
pencil
55 x 35.5cm
DCM

122 *Death of Agammemnon*
circa 1974
pencil
55 x 36.7cm
DCM

123 *Theseus and the Minotaur*
circa 1974
pencil
51.5 x 34cm
DCM

124 *Walking Madonna* circa 1980
watercolour
76.9 x 57cm
SFL

125 *Dog* 1981
pencil
74.7 x 55cm
DCM

126 *Striding Man* 1983
pencil
77.3 x 57cm
SFL

127 *Melancholy Man* circa 1981
pencil
96.7 x 67.4cm
DCM

128 *Horse* 1982
pencil
100 x 70cm
SFL

129 *Oedipus* circa 1983
etching
76 x 60cm
DCM

130 *Kalydonian Boar* circa 1983
etching
76 x 60cm
DCM

131 *Apollo* circa 1983
etching
76 x 60cm
DCM

132 *Ganymede* circa 1983
etching
76 x 60cm
DCM

133 *Bellerophon* circa 1983
etching
76 x 60cm
DCM

134 *Seated Man I* 1986
pencil
184 x 122.5cm
DCM

135 *Seated Man II* circa 1985
pencil
100 x 70.4cm
SFL

136 *Baboon* circa 1986
coloured etching
38 x 36.8cm
DCM

137 *Baboon* circa 1986
coloured etching
38 x 36.8cm
DCM

138 *Tiger* 1986
coloured etching
35.5 x 28.1cm
DCM

139 *Tiger* circa 1986
coloured etching
35.5 x 28.1cm
DCM

140 *Wounded Horse* 1987
gouache
72.3 x 52.7cm
DCM

141 *Head* circa 1988
screenprint
103 x 71cm
DCM

142 *Horse's Head* circa 1989
screenprint
95.5 x 68.6cm
DCM

143 *Running Dog* circa 1989
screenprint
98 x 71cm
DCM

144 *Baboon and Man* 1990
gouache
166.6 x 107.8cm
DCM

145 *Baboon and Man* 1990
gouache
117.2 x 117.2cm
SFL and DCM

146 *Green Man* 1991
pencil
101.2 x 68.5cm
SFL

Afterword

The address given

by Brian Phelan

at the memorial for

Dame Elisabeth Frink

at St James's

Church Piccadilly,

21 September, 1993

It seems to me no accident that in the last years of her life Lis became fascinated by the legend of the *Green Man*, that ancient and continuously re-appearing symbol of regeneration and birth.

It was always life and living she cared about, however difficult and distressing that might sometimes be. Death was certainly to be recognised, looked at, raged at, but not acquiesced to.

Her *Madonna* at Salisbury is not a woman crushed by sorrow and death. She is not nobly suffering but strides forward, affirming life, interested to see what lies in the future while the understanding of the past is etched clearly, and deeply in the lines of her face.

So for me today is a celebration. A hooley. A celebration of an extraordinary and unique person who has touched all our lives. A woman and artist of great generosity, daring, bravery and phenomenal energy. She flung herself at life and at work. Her energy and love embraced us all and enriched our lives.

The first time I went with my family to spend summer with Lis in France we arrived at Corbes in the early evening after the long drive from Calais. Immediately the choice was pastis or champagne or, most likely, both. Then she was at the barbecue gesticulating with a collection of skewers that would have made Errol Flynn blanch. She had taken a house for us and as it got dark I worried how we would ever find it. It was simple, of course, we would follow Lis. She yelled for her dog Pollux, they both dived into a battered vehicle and took off down the twisting road to the river. By the time she started across the bridge with no sides I was behind her. Even in the daylight when I had become familiar with it, that bridge worried me. Arriving at it for the first time, in the dark doing 50 miles an hour, as her rearlights disappeared was to experience Lis's contradictory sense of time. Finding her again,

Elisabeth Frink and Alex Csárky

75

on the track up to Madame Meyer's meant saying goodbye to caution.

Seeing that French hill farmer's wife greet Lis was to witness how she affected people. We were hours late, we had to go further up the hill to our rented home but Madame Meyer was only delighted and pleased to see and talk to Madame Lis.

The two women walked up the mountain, lit by my headlights. We watched Lis listen with interest to the vagaries and difficulties of producing cheese from such a difficult and, yet, magnificent herd of goats that were Madame Meyer's lot. Suddenly there was all the time in the world.

That was the first of many wonderful summers we spent at Corbes with Lis and Ted. She had the gift to make every occasion special. Shopping in Anduze with a café stop after was as memorable as the days of the grape harvest in the late summer. Whatever you shared with her became a heightened experience, ...to be savoured because she was at the centre of it. She made you look and be aware, not by pointing things out but by the act of living it herself.

In her attitude to people she was the truest democrat I have known. She did not respond to the fame or status of a person, or the lack of it. She looked at people, listened to them, then made up her mind. She played no games, she was herself with everybody and that is what people responded to and loved her for. She was created a Dame by her country but she was also a 'dame' in the best American sense of the word.

Above all, the energy was in her work. To wake up after a late night at Corbes and see Lis, shortly after dawn, make her way across the track to her stone wall studio was to understand her fundamental urge and necessity to create.

I went into her studio one morning to find her staring at the work in progress with total concentration. She muttered 'it's not right' picked up a two pound lump hammer and went at it like a Mayo navvy on piece work. Plaster flew all over the studio. It was the most unnerving and exhilarating thing to watch. I said 'I hope you know what you're doing.' But of course she did. She mixed up some fresh plaster and I sat there watching her create a more perfect work of art. I consider it one of the most privileged mornings of my life.

She was wonderfully gregarious, equally delighted by new people as old friends. They were to be looked after, victualled, wined, questioned, stimulated and encouraged. Most especially young artists. She gave them her time unstintingly. There are many artists working today who were given faith in themselves and their talent by her generosity, support and encouragement.

But above all she herself was the consummate artist. Her work was her life. Her turning down the historic offer to become the first woman President of the Royal Academy was because it would take time from her work. I can think of few people so centred.

She loved the men in her life. She loved her family and she loved her friends. She was not one for over-articulating this, she simply expressed it in everything she did. Except for her joy in Tully. At the drop of her hat or, latterly, her turban, she would talk about her grandchild.

She was outraged by injustice. Her feeling for the downtrodden, the tortured, the cruelly treated, powerless people of our world was acute, deeply felt and totally unromantic. It is all there in her work, alarmingly, in the *Goggle Heads* and sadly, bravely and hopefully in the series of heads, the *Tributes,* done for Amnesty.

She also had a fine indignation about what happened to her own country in the Eighties, not just to artists but to the sensibilities of ordinary people.

She exhibited amazing bravery and grace in the last few months, always planning new work, thinking about the future and above all, the figure for Liverpool. To be with her while she worked on it, discussed it, was to be with a person who was only interested in life. Although she did not make it to the unveiling she was there, in the work, and she will be there for centuries.

She loved Dorset and she loved country living and that she shared, for years of great pleasure with Alex, who loved his horses, his dogs, Woolland and, above all, his 'girl'.

I do not understand the scientific explanation of the black hole in space but I do, now, understand the black emotional hole that has appeared in my life.

But the hole is not so black. It is filled with colours and shapes, with running men and beautiful animals and above all it echoes with that wonderful bark and hoot of laughter that engulfed you when Lis was at her best and happiest.

Elisabeth Frink:
sculptures, graphic works, textiles

This catalogue is published to
accompany exhibitions organised by
The Salisbury Festival with
The Edwin Young Trust, Salisbury
and Dorset County Museum, Dorchester

Elisabeth Frink:
a certain unexpectedness
Salisbury Library and Galleries
10 May - 7 June 1997
Salisbury Cathedral
22 May - 19 June 1997

Elisabeth Frink:
man and the animal world
Dorset County Museum
28 June - 23 August 1997

Edited and prepared by
Annette Downing

Designed by
Pip Paton-Walker

Printed by
Nuffield Press

Type set in
Monotype Gill Sans

Published by
The Edwin Young Trust,
Wiltshire County Council
and Salisbury Festival

ISBN 0-86080-417-8

Illustrated works are copyright
The Estate of Dame Elisabeth Frink 1994

We would like to thank the following
for the use of their photographs:
The Estate of Dame Elisabeth Frink
David Buckland
Jorge Lewinski
John Morely
Morris Singer Foundry
AC Cooper
Peter Kinnear
Joe Low
Brian Seed
R Sloman
John Timbers

All exhibited works courtesy
of the lenders

Front cover shows the
Walking Madonna and Salisbury Cathedral
photograph by Jorge Lewinski

opposite, Woolland, with *Riace* figures
in foreground, early 1990s